THE IRISH POTATO FAMINE

BY JILL SHERMAN

A CAUSE-AND-EFFECT
INVESTIGATION

CAUSE + EFFECT
DISASTERS

LERNER PUBLICATIONS ◆ MINNEAPOLIS

Lerner Publications Company
A division of Lerner Publishing Group, Inc.
241 First Avenue North
Minneapolis, MN 55401 USA

For reading levels and more information, look up this title at www.lernerbooks.com.

Content Consultant: Professor Christine Kinealy, Director, Ireland's Great Hunger Institute, Quinnipiac University

Library of Congress Cataloging-in-Publication Data

Names: Sherman, Jill., author.
Title: The Irish Potato Famine : a cause-and-effect investigation / by Jill Sherman.
Description: Minneapolis : Lerner Publications, [2017] | Series: Cause-and-effect disasters | Audience: Ages 9-12. | Audience: Grades 4 to 6. | Includes bibliographical references and index.
Identifiers: LCCN 2016008878 (print) | LCCN 2016022998 (ebook) | ISBN 9781512411195 (lb : alk. paper) | ISBN 9781512411317 (eb pdf)
Subjects: LCSH: Late blight of potato—Ireland—Juvenile literature. | Famines—Ireland—History— 19th century—Juvenile literature. | Disaster victims—Ireland—History—19th century—Juvenile literature. | Ireland—History—Famine, 1845-1852—Juvenile literature. | Ireland—Emigration and immigration—History—19th century—Juvenile literature.
Classification: LCC DA950.7 .S54 2017 (print) | LCC DA950.7 (ebook) | DDC 941.5081—dc23

LC record available at https://lccn.loc.gov/2016008878

Manufactured in the United States of America
1 – VP – 7/15/16

TABLE OF CONTENTS

THE COMING STORM

1

Lush green landscapes and rolling meadows fill the Irish countryside. The country is well known for its natural beauty. But when French traveler Gustave de Beaumont arrived in 1838, he noticed something else. Ireland was in stark poverty. "Misery, naked and famishing [starvation] . . . it is the first thing you see when you land on the Irish coast, and from that moment it ceases not to be present to your view," he wrote.

Ireland came fully under English control as part of the United Kingdom in 1801.

De Beaumont saw swarms of poor people in the cities. They wore ragged clothing. They begged for food. Traveling into the countryside, he saw rundown one-room cabins. They were made of mud. There were no windows or chimneys. Inside, several generations of a family lived together. They had no furniture. They shared a single straw mattress.

Farmers, cottiers, and landless laborers made up Ireland's large working class. Farmers often had several acres of land to farm. Cottiers usually had less than an acre. Some of them worked for farmers with larger crops to harvest. Landless laborers were the poorest. They did not grow their own crops.

Gustave de Beaumont wrote about his observations in an 1839 book, *Ireland: Social, Political, and Religious.*

5

Most of the farmers were Catholics. They did not own the land they lived on. Rather, they rented it, mostly from Protestant landlords. Many of the landlords lived in England. To make matters more complicated, the farmers did not pay their landlords directly. Instead, the landlords rented the land to middlemen. These men were usually Protestant too. The middlemen divided the land into small plots. They rented these plots to the Irish farmers for higher prices than they paid. The farmers paid the middlemen. The middlemen kept some money. They paid the landowners the rest.

Nearly all of a farm's earnings went to the landlords and middlemen. If a farmer somehow made a profit or came into some money, it was wise to hide it. The farmer would not want the landlord to know that the family had new clothes or a repaired roof. Any sign that they had money would be a reason for the landlord to raise the rent even higher.

The relationships between farmers and landlords were tense. And this was not just because of unfair rent increases. Most of the

Irish families lived in small cottages and rented their land. Reproductions and ruins of these homes can be seen in Ireland today.

NUTRITIONAL VALUE OF A POTATO

WATER
224 grams

CARBOHYDRATE	FAT	NIACIN
63 grams	0.4 grams	4.2 milligrams
PROTEIN	**PHOSPHORUS**	**IRON**
7 grams	209 milligrams	3.2 milligrams
FIBER	**VITAMIN C**	**THIAMINE**
7 grams	28.7 milligrams	0.2 milligrams
POTASSIUM	**CALCIUM**	**RIBOFLAVIN**
1,600 milligrams	44.8 milligrams	0.1 milligrams

English landowners had acquired their land from their ancestors. Those ancestors had taken the Irish land during invasions and wars. In many cases, the land had been taken from the same Irish families who were now paying to rent it. Irish farmers did not like the system. Many believed that the land rightfully belonged to their families. But the landowners didn't see it that way. Under English law, the land belonged to the landowners. That meant they owned whatever profits the land produced. To squeeze out more money, middlemen divided the land into smaller and smaller plots. At the same time they also raised the rent. By 1845 farmers typically had only 1 to 5 acres (0.4 to 2 hectares) of land.

This system worked only because of the potato crop. Potatoes thrive in Ireland's climate. They grow well even in the rocky, poor soil. And they are nutritious. Potatoes are a good source of potassium, vitamin C, and fiber.

Potatoes also have a large harvest. Irish farmers could grow enough to feed their families. They only needed a small plot of land. By growing potatoes on 1 acre (0.4 ha) of land, a typical Irish family could eat for an entire year. They could also feed their livestock the potato scraps. Farmers would have needed three times as much land to survive on if not for the potato. The rest of their farmland was for crops they could sell, such as oats and grain. That money was used to pay the rent.

Potatoes became Ireland's most important crop. By 1845 about one-third of Ireland's farmland was used for potato crops. And farmers mostly all planted the same variety. They were called Lumpers. Lumpers were not the most nutritious kind of potato, but they had a large harvest.

Irish farmers planted their potatoes in March. They harvested in September or October. They then buried the harvested potatoes in pits. The potatoes kept until July the next year—just before the next harvest. Families may not have had much to eat during the month of August. Still, the potatoes kept them well fed for the rest of the year. Some of Ireland's poorest people ate nothing but potatoes.

The Lumper potato variety arrived in Ireland after 1810. It grew well even in poor soil.

In the growing season of 1845, more potatoes were planted than usual. Besides growing on farmland, potatoes grew on hillsides and in bogs across Ireland. Crops had failed in years past because of disease and poor weather. So the crop of 1845 was closely watched. The weather alternated between sun and cold, heavy rains. But the fields turned green. There were rumors in August that crops had failed in southern England. But Ireland was more than 100 miles (160 kilometers) away. In September, the harvest began. The potatoes looked edible. But within days they turned slimy, black, and smelly. What would this mean for the people of Ireland?

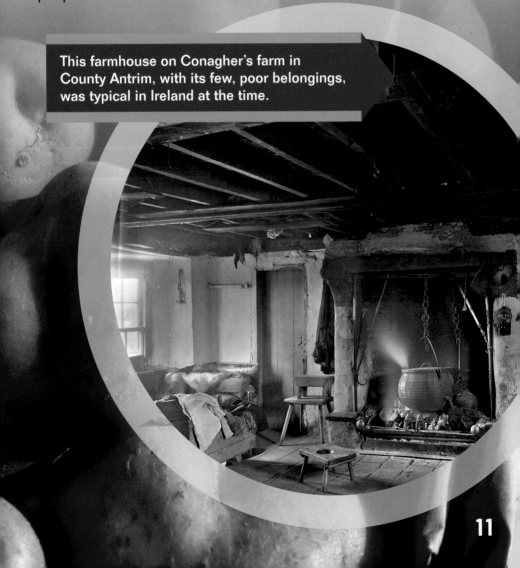

This farmhouse on Conagher's farm in County Antrim, with its few, poor belongings, was typical in Ireland at the time.

THE POTATO BLIGHT

In 1845 the black, rotten potato crops were completely inedible. Irish farmers with blighted crops were in trouble. Because potatoes were their largest source of food, poor people were left with little to eat. If they had to buy food for their families, they would not be able to pay the rent they owed on their farms.

The blight was widespread. But crops had failed in the past. Between 1800 and 1845 Ireland had seen sixteen food shortages. The 1845 blight was the first shortage to affect all of Ireland. The British government knew about the failed potato crop. They sent experts to study the problem. The group thought that Ireland was likely to lose half of its potato crop. But Parliament, the group of

Blight starts as a dark patch on the potato's skin. The inside rots soon after.

British lawmakers, wasn't terribly worried. After all, Ireland had recovered from blight before. Parliament did not want to get too involved in Irish affairs. Most people in England thought that the Irish should deal with the problem on their own. They thought the Irish would have a lean year, but the problem would be fixed by the next year's harvest.

Even so, a few temporary programs were created to help. Most notable was Prime Minister Robert Peel's repeal of the Corn Laws. These laws put high import tariffs on grain.

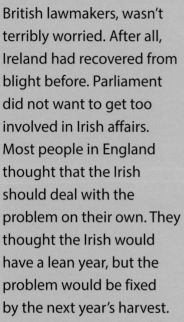

Peel's repeal of the Corn Laws was the most controversial decision of his career.

13

The tariffs were originally meant to protect British sellers from outside competition. Peel had wanted to repeal the Corn Laws for some time. He thought they were bad for the British economy. The blight gave him an added reason. In spring of 1846, Peel allowed the import of grain. By that summer, he had officially repealed the Corn Laws. With the repeal, inexpensive grain could now be imported to Ireland. Peel purchased maize, a hard, cheap kind of corn, directly from the United States. Unfortunately, before maize can be eaten, it must be heavily processed. Ireland had very few mills that could do this. Mills that received the heavy, pebble-like maize soon discovered one grinding was not enough. The maize had to be ground twice. No matter how much maize was imported, only a limited amount could be made ready to eat. Maize imports did add some grain to the food supply. But it was not enough to be very helpful.

Once the maize was ground into meal, it sold for a penny a pound (0.45 kilograms). But even with lower prices, many couldn't afford to buy it. The blighted potato crop meant they had very little money. It also wasn't as nutritious as potatoes. And the Irish weren't used to digesting maize. Those who did eat it often suffered from diarrhea and scurvy. Scurvy causes bleeding gums and keeps wounds from healing. Disease spread. This strained the already hungry population. Corn would not be the answer to Ireland's problems.

The repeal of the Corn Laws was an ineffective and unpopular act. Many British government officials disagreed with the decision. They disliked that they no longer had control of the grain market. Peel was forced to resign his position as prime minister in 1846.

Charles Edward Trevelyan, who was then responsible for famine policy, quickly ended the sale of maize. Trevelyan supported Parliament's hands-off policy toward Ireland. He worried that if England got too involved, the Irish would begin to rely on government handouts. According to Trevelyan, helping the Irish brought "the risk of paralyzing all private enterprise." But Trevelyan did support some aid programs. The Soup Kitchen Act paid for temporary free soup kitchens. A public works program gave jobs to poor Irish farmers. But the pay was very low.

Overall, the Irish could not expect much help from the British government. This attitude was partly due to English prejudice against Irish Catholics. Some English thought of

Many Irish people did not like Trevelyan. They thought he should have done more to help.

the Irish as lazy. Potato farming required periods of hard labor, but the crops didn't need much tending. So Irish farmers alternated between periods of hard work and rest. This lifestyle didn't match up with the English idea of good workers.

By late 1845 Ireland had lost about half of its potato crop to the blight. The English still believed the food shortage would not last. They thought that if the Irish people needed more help, Ireland should use its own tax revenue. But wages for Irish workers were very low. Taxes on these wages would not support big aid projects.

Irish farmers had to work hard to prepare the rocky land for planting, but many British still assumed the Irish were lazy.

Irish farmers set aside potatoes to use as seeds for the next season's crop.

The Irish made it through the year after the blight. Most lived on maize imports and what they could salvage from their crops. Some sold their livestock and their belongings to buy food. Many fell behind on the rent. Farmers were weary from the difficult year. But they managed to plant the next season's potatoes. By the end of the summer in 1846 the new crop was ready to harvest. Everyone was counting on it to be free of blight.

THE GREAT HUNGER

The blight returned with the 1846
potato crops. The last crop had
been so devastated that many farmers
had no seeds except those from the blighted
potatoes. No one had a scientific understanding of the disease.
Even the British experts had recommended planting these seeds.
Unfortunately, this only extended the blight.

**Potatoes grow
under the ground.**

IRELAND'S POTATO CROP, 1845–1848

POTATOES PRODUCED IN THOUSANDS OF TONS

- 12,000
- 10,000
- 8,000
- 6,000
- 4,000
- 2,000
- 0

10,063 — 1845
2,999 — 1846
2,046 — 1847
3,077 — 1848

YEAR

Blight is a disease caused by the fungus *Phytophthora infestans*. The spores spread on the wind, infecting the leaves of other plants. Potato plants have tubers, a system of roots, underground. New buds sprout from the tubers. Blight spores can be washed into the soil, infecting the tubers. Crops are more likely to suffer from blight in seasons of heavy rainfall.

This second year of blight was much worse. The famine took hold. The Irish later called the years 1845 to 1852 the Great Hunger. One Catholic priest in Ireland described people "on the fences of their decaying gardens, wringing their hands and wailing bitterly." John Doyle's family suffered through the famine. He remembered their stories of how "the people ate crabapples and holly-berries and the leaves of the crabtree. They climbed trees for nuts. . . . Many were so weak they fell out of the trees and were killed."

Thousands died from hunger and disease. The already weakened Irish faced epidemics of typhoid and cholera. People with these diseases suffered from fever, stomach pains, and diarrhea. Scurvy became even more of a problem.

In the midst of all this suffering, the Irish began to examine the actions of the British government. Food continued to be exported out of Ireland. British owners of Irish land were still entitled to the crops grown on that land. Their businesses relied on these crops. And British policy did not prevent the export. Starving Irish people became furious as they watched boatloads of grain depart from their docks for England. Food riots erupted at ports such as Youghal and Dungarvan in southeast Ireland.

Starving Irish people raid a government store of potatoes in the harbor city of Galway.

23

In response, the British assigned military officers to protect and escort ships in Irish harbors.

To provide relief, the British government created the Irish Poor Law Extension Act in June 1847. The act made landowners in Ireland responsible for famine relief. It was no longer the responsibility of the British government to help. The public works projects and soup kitchens had ended. These had been meant as only temporary relief. The Irish Poor Law would take over.

But landlords weren't able to help much. Many were deeply in debt. With public works projects shut down, many Irish workers were suddenly unemployed. The 1847 potato crop had come in healthy, at last. But few farmers had been able to plant that year.

An Irish family sits outside their cottage in County Donegal with their belongings after being evicted.

To avoid starvation, many had eaten the potatoes that would have been kept aside for planting. Others were too weak from hunger to plant a large crop. The 1847 harvest was just a quarter of its normal size. So even without the blight, the famine remained dire. One descendant of famine survivors recalled, "The people used to gather leaves of dandelions and boil them. Then they strained the water off and made gruel by putting meal [coarse flour] into the water."

Under the burden of the Irish Poor Law, some landlords could no longer afford the taxes on small properties. Many chose to evict, or kick out, their tenants. Eviction was a complicated process. It required a legal judgment. If the judge ruled in the landlord's favor, the family had to move out of their home.

A large group of Irish people waits to be let into a workhouse in 1846.

So when Irish farmers were faced with eviction, many chose to flee rather than appear in court. More than 250,000 people were formally evicted. But the total number of people forced to leave their homes was closer to 500,000.

Former farmers sought relief in workhouses. These shelters were often the last resort for those in need. They offered food and housing to those able to work. For men, this often meant breaking stones that would be used to build roads. Women might help with cooking and cleaning. Workers had to put in ten-hour days.

By 1847 there were about 130 workhouses. They housed about 100,000 people in total. This number increased throughout the famine. Men and women had separate housing. This meant families had to split up. The workhouses were dirty and overcrowded. Disease spread.

William Keane remembered his family's stories about workhouses, saying, "[Poor people] were badly treated in the workhouse. The food was poor and stingy. Those over them had no feeling for them." Some workers even preferred prison to living in workhouses. Even so, the workhouses were so full that many people were turned away.

After a season of heavy rain, the blight returned again in 1848. By this point, some British people were angry that the Irish had continued to rely on potatoes. The farmers may have wanted to plant other crops. But they often didn't have money to purchase seeds. They planted the crops they could, which were potatoes.

Rather than wait for things to improve, many Irish left the country. Some left for England, making their way to Liverpool on England's west coast. Many Irish already lived there. Others sailed overseas. They hoped for new opportunities in British North America or the United States. But the journeys could be rough. Ships bound for Canada were often overcrowded and poorly built. They became known as "coffin ships." The trip could take as long as three months to complete. Thousands died before they reached land. Those who survived the journey had little to eat. They often got typhus, dysentery, and other diseases.

Over the course of the famine, Ireland saw a dramatic drop in its population. The estimated death toll was 1 million. An additional 2 million people emigrated out of the country. And Ireland still had more hardships left to face.

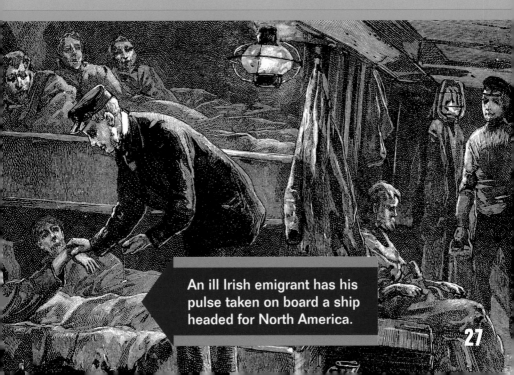

An ill Irish emigrant has his pulse taken on board a ship headed for North America.

AFTER THE FAMINE

4

Most historians agree that the famine had reached its end by 1852. But hunger remained a problem for years. Even though the blight had ended, the Irish economy had suffered greatly.

Ireland's population had been booming before the famine. The country could have had 9 million people by 1851. Instead, Ireland's population was devastated. Ireland was home to just 6.5 million people in that year.

The people who survived had scraped by during the famine years. They had no money or energy to help revive their country. Few Irish farmers could pay their rent or produce a large potato crop. Without this income, landowners also fell deeper in debt. Many began to sell off their estates.

This illustration of Irish emigrants boarding a ship appeared in the *Illustrated London News* in 1850.

POPULATION OF IRELAND

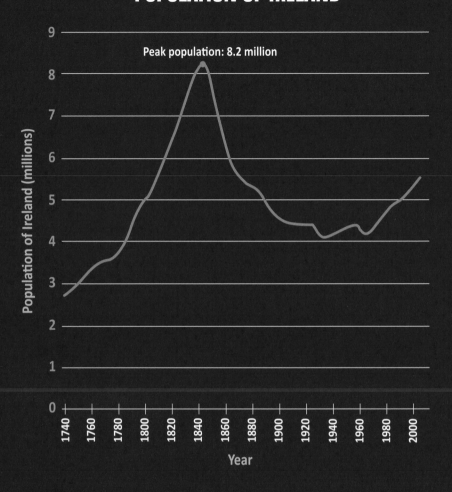

Peak population: 8.2 million

Population of Ireland (millions)

Year

In 1849, as more bankrupt landowners sold their estates, land prices dropped. Wealthy Irish farmers and some British businessmen saw a new opportunity. They began to snatch up land at bargain prices. They immediately increased the rent on the tenant farmers or evicted them. Those who could not afford the rent were left homeless. Their homes were knocked down to make way for more cattle-grazing land.

Irish farmers and laborers began to resist. The Land League was led by Charles Stewart Parnell. It organized boycotts. It pressured Parliament for change. The league had three aims. Called the "three Fs," they were fair rent, fixed tenure, and the free sale of land. The long-term goal was for Irish farmers to own their land. Eventually, the Irish made progress. The Land Purchase Act of 1903 made the landlord-tenant system more fair for tenants.

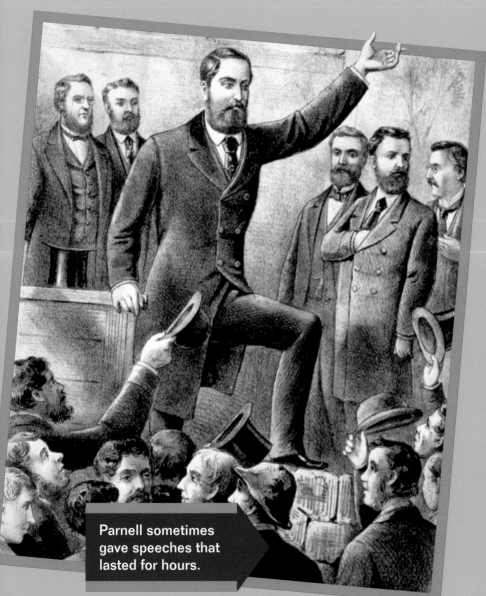

Parnell sometimes gave speeches that lasted for hours.

PATH OF THE POTATO BLIGHT

CANADA

UNITED
STATES

Early 1800s

MEXICO

P. infestans origin

Still, farm life never returned to what it had been before the famine. The birth rate had declined. Irish people continued to emigrate. The population dropped steadily until the 1960s. By then, the economy relied more heavily on industrial work. People began to settle in Ireland's cities. Abandoned villages and vacant land, especially in western Ireland, remain visible today.

IRELAND

1845

N
W ← • → E
S

Atlantic
Ocean

Everyone knew that blight caused the food shortage. But it took
modern researchers to track down the precise strain. The blight
was originally native to Mexico. Researchers say the fungus likely
traveled north to the United States or Canada first. Then it crossed
the Atlantic to Ireland.

Although the blight caused Ireland's food shortage, Britain's policies added to the problems. Britain took a largely hands-off approach toward the famine. Even while people in Ireland were starving, Britain continued to allow the export of food. The government made some efforts toward relief with soup kitchens, public works projects, and the repeal of the Corn Laws. But these weak policies did not help much. Stronger action by the British government could have prevented some suffering.

The famine changed Ireland's history. It had a deep and long-lasting effect on all parts of Ireland. Today, Ireland has regained economic stability. The Republic of Ireland is now an independent nation. The population has passed 4.5 million and is slowly growing. Northern Ireland is part of the United Kingdom and has a population of 1.8 million. Ireland is no longer a suffering country. But the pain of the famine will always be remembered.

Ruins such as these in County Kerry still dot the Irish countryside.

CAUSE

Potatoes thrive in Ireland and are a good source of nutrition for poor families.

In 1845 blight hits some potato crops, making the potatoes inedible.

Blighted potatoes are used for seeds for the next year's crop.

The British, not wanting the Irish to rely on government aid and holding prejudiced views about Irish people, provide only minimal relief.

The British government turns over the responsibility for famine relief to Protestant landowners who are already struggling financially.

EFFECT

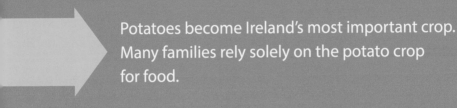

Potatoes become Ireland's most important crop. Many families rely solely on the potato crop for food.

Some Irish families are left with little to eat and become unable to pay their rent.

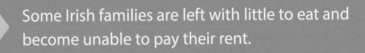

Blight continues for a second year in 1846.

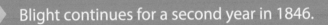

Many Irish people starve during the Great Hunger, 1845–1852.

Landowners evict their tenants. Many Irish people starve, leave the country, or end up in workhouses.

Glossary

blight: a plant disease

climate: the typical weather conditions of a place over many years

evict: to remove a person from occupying a property

famine: a great food shortage

landlord: the owner of land or houses that are rented to another person

middlemen: dealers who act as go-betweens for two different parties

prejudice: judging someone without cause, often based on stereotypes

public works: projects, such as schools, highways, or docks, that are constructed with public funds for community use

scurvy: a disease caused by lack of vitamin C

tariffs: government taxes on imported or exported goods

tenure: the right to use property

Source Notes

4   Ciarán Ó Murchadha, *The Great Famine: Ireland's Agony* (New York: Bloomsbury Publishing, 2011), 1.

16 Philip Gavin, "Irish Potato Famine," *The History Place*, accessed February 19, 2016, http://www.historyplace.com/worldhistory/famine/hunger.htm.

21 Michael F. J. McDonnell, *Ireland and the Home Rule Movement* (Dublin: Maunsel & Co., 1908), 42.

21 Cathal Poirteir, *Famine Echoes: Folk Memories of the Great Irish Famine* (Dublin: Gill and MacMillan Ltd., 1995), IFC 1075: 200–22.

25   Cathal Poirteir, *Famine Echoes: Folk Memories of the Great Irish Famine* (Dublin: Gill and MacMillan Ltd., 1995), IFC 1075: 520–35.

26 Cathal Poirteir, *Famine Echoes: Folk Memories of the Great Irish Famine* (Dublin: Gill and MacMillan Ltd., 1995), IFC 1075: 484–98.

Selected Bibliography

Donnelly, Jim. "The Irish Famine." *BBC History.* February 17, 2011. http://www.bbc.co.uk/history/british/victorians/famine_01.shtml#top.

Gavin, Philip. "Irish Potato Famine." *The History Place.* Accessed February 19, 2016. http://www.historyplace.com/worldhistory/famine/hunger.htm.

McDonnell, Michael F. J. *Ireland and the Home Rule Movement.* Dublin: Maunsel & Co., 1908.

Ó Murchadha, Ciarán. *The Great Famine: Ireland's Agony.* New York: Bloomsbury Publishing, 2011.

Further Information

Books

Bartoletti, Susan Campbell. *Black Potatoes: The Story of the Great Irish Famine 1845–1850.* New York: HMH Books for Young Readers, 2014. Discover the story of the Irish potato famine through the stories of the people who lived through it.

Blashfield, Jean F. *Ireland: Enchantment of the World.* New York: Scholastic, 2014. Learn about the history and culture of Ireland.

Lyons, Mary E. *Feed the Children First: Irish Memories of the Great Hunger.* New York: Atheneum Books for Young Readers, 2012. Get a close-up look at the Great Hunger through first-person accounts.

Websites

Ireland's Great Hunger Institute
http://www.quinnipiac.edu/institutes-and-centers/irelands-great-hunger-institute
Learn more about the Great Hunger and its effects on Irish culture and history.

National Geographic Kids: Ireland
http://kids.nationalgeographic.com/explore/countries/ireland
Discover more about Ireland, including the country's flag, geography, and history.

Strokestown Park: Irish National Famine Museum
http://www.strokestownpark.ie/famine-museum
Watch a video to discover the museum's artifacts and displays on the Irish potato famine.

Index

Photo Credits